Who Really Sends the Missionary?

By

MICHAEL C. GRIFFITHS

General Director
Overseas Missionary Fellowship

MOODY PRESS
CHICAGO

Published in the U.K. by OMF Books
under the title *Get Involved in Missions!*

© 1972, Overseas Missionary Fellowship

MOODY PRESS EDITION, 1974

ISBN: 0-8024-9498-6

All scripture quotations in this book are from
the New American Standard Bible.

The selection of this version of the Bible for
use in this publication does not necessarily
imply publisher endorsement of the version in
its entirety.

Printed in the United States of America

Contents

Introduction

IT MIGHT SEEM CYNICAL to say that the main interest of missions in churches and their ministers today seems to be—money. Most would agree that the relationship between home churches and foreign missions is under strain. They have not divorced each other, but, frequently, they seem estranged, formal, and failing to communicate with each other. Like nagging wives, the missionary societies complain that the churches are not supplying them with enough men or enough money. For their part, on the other hand, the churches, like disappointed husbands, complain that the missionary societies have become jaded and unattractive. How have we gotten ourselves into such a mess?

I would suggest it is because the present shallow and superficial relationship between congregations and the work of mission societies is a parody of the vital relationship that existed in New Testament times. An examination of the biblical passages concerning the relationships of Barnabas, Paul, Mark, Silas, and Timothy with the churches of Jerusalem, Antioch, and Lystra will show us why.

A recent statistical survey and report by the

Evangelical Missionary Alliance in Britain comments, "Peaceful co-existence rather than vital co-operation might well sum up the usual relationship between the missionary and the ordinary church member."[1] We all want to see a vital and exciting relationship restored between churches and mission societies, and this can be effected practically where there is increased living contact between individual Christians and individual missionaries. The survey concludes that the occasional, fleeting visits of missionaries to address formal meetings are insufficient.

From the USA, Ian Hay speaks of "the tired shop-worn image which is displayed in our sending churches,"[2] while from Britain, we read,

> Nothing could be worse than the present arrangement whereby in many evangelical churches, a number of different missionary societies, chosen without any coordination or strategy, send representatives, leave collecting boxes and distribute magazines. The result is a confused situation which makes it virtually impossible for the members of the church to get a comprehensive or balanced world view; moreover it is wasteful of time and money spent in travelling on the part of missionary society staffs. Where the church supports one denominational society the lack of balance is in some ways even greater, since interest is confined to that particular denomination, and to those areas of the world where it happens to have repre-

sentatives; the denomination, as much as the gospel becomes a focus of concern.[3]

In North America, ministers are disenchanted with the stream of expensive self-promotion materials pouring through their mailboxes. Constant requests come from missionary societies and missionaries wanting to occupy the minister's pulpit for deputation, in order to plug their own work and to raise money for their own support. Dr. J. Robertson McQuilkin points out "how easy it is for missions to become mission-centred, considering the church a source of money and the (Bible) school the source of recruits." Is there no more satisfying or more scriptural way of involving congregations in missions?

Deputation is so dull. Missions are not helped by their old-fashioned image, with their exhibition sideshows of dog-eared leaflets and anthropological bric-a-brac. The old traditional lantern lecture, usually a pious travelogue with shots of ecclesiastical buildings, group photographs of curiously garbed congregations, and action shots of the intrepid missionary on the trail, has become the greatly improved slide series, made even more contemporary (and more condensed!) by using a prerecorded soundtrack as an audio-visual, but this cannot be relied upon necessarily to enthuse the congregation as a whole with the fading attractiveness of missions. Exaggerated rumors of their anticipated demise are also not especially helpful!

In a mature relationship, it ought not to be necessary for the mission to have constantly to persuade the church to remember the importance of its partner. If a real and vital relationship can be reestablished, then the constant clamoring for attention and nagging for money can disappear, as churches and missions reciprocally enjoy a greater sense of mutual responsibility in doing things together. We long to see churches afire with enthusiasm for the greatest possible personal involvement in taking the good news of the Lord Jesus to those who have never heard it.

How often, following a missionary deputation weekend, have we asked ourselves, "Is there no better way than this?"

I am convinced there is. Thus this booklet.

The following suggestions have been aired and discussed with several groups of ministers in different countries and have met with an encouraging reception, so that it seems worth trying to share them with a wider audience. Some of the material in this first section also appears in *Give Up Your Small Ambitions* (Moody Press, 1971), a book for potential missionary candidates, but it seems worthwhile to produce something briefer for congregational consumption. Though the author is associated with one particular board, Overseas Missionary Fellowship, the suggestions

aim at a pattern which could be mutually beneficial to all congregations and all societies. It is
deliberately addressed to the situation in general,
and therefore its attitudes toward financial policy,
deputation, promotion, and the like, presupposes
a much wider one than solely the particular interests of OMF as only one of a large number of
societies.

1

Who Selects the New Missionary?

Ministers and congregations have the chief responsibility for the selecting and sending of new missionaries.

MISSIONARY SOCIETIES have been forced, in recent years, to a biblical reevaluation of the importance of the *receiving church* on the field. The traditionally independent and individualistic approach of the so-called faith mission is changing. There is, correspondingly, a fresh realization of the biblical relationship between the *sending church* and missions. The so-called faith policy, with its valued stress upon "dependence on God alone," may have been, to some extent, responsible for a neglect of the proper intimacy between sending congregations and missions. Kerry Lovering writes, "The scriptural role of the local church as the sending authority and financial base for world evangelism needs to be brought back into clearer focus."[1]

So often, the missionary societies have gone to the Bible colleges to recruit missionaries, and while this is perfectly understandable, it would be more appropriate if we came to you in the local churches.

> Generally all of these young people contacted and challenged are related to local churches, and in the final analysis it will be the local church which must be spiritually and financially involved.[2]

THE BIBLICAL RELATIONSHIP

One of the most intriguing aspects of the Acts passages is the total absence of any appeals for volunteers. I was extremely embarrassed when asked at a large convention recently to give an appeal for young people to come forward as volunteers for missions. My text, as it happened, was Acts 11:22, "They sent Barnabas." The passage indicates that it was the congregation in Jerusalem which selected and sent one of its own most gifted members to Antioch. The Holy Spirit, the Author of Scripture, chooses to say nothing about appeals for volunteers or Barnabas's subjective sense of call, but focuses attention upon the Jerusalem congregation's corporate responsibility for the objective selecting and sending of an individual. It is significant that in all the subsequent "sendings" of missionaries in Acts, the emphasis made by Scripture is never upon an individual volunteering or upon his own subjective sense of call, but always upon the initiative of others. Saul goes to

Antioch because Barnabas takes him there (Ac 11:25-26). It is the whole group of prophets and teachers in Antioch to whom the Holy Spirit says, "Set apart for Me Barnabas and Saul for the work to which I have called them" (Ac 13:1-4). Later, when Barnabas and Paul parted company, we are told that Barnabas "took Mark" (Ac 15:39) and Paul "chose Silas" (Ac 15:40) "and departed, being committed by the brethren to the grace of the Lord." Subsequently, Paul "wanted" Timothy "to go with him" (Ac 16:3), though we are pointedly reminded that "he was well spoken of by the brethren who were in Lystra and Iconium," so that the congregations then were consulted and involved in his going out.

Whereas we seem to have emphasized exclusively the individual's subjective sense of a highly personal call of God, and often reinforced this by emotional appeals for individuals to volunteer, the New Testament by contrast stresses either the corporate initiative of congregations or the informed initiative of missionaries in selecting suitable people.

The volunteer system is thus suspect on *biblical grounds*. It cannot be justified from the New Testament, and the best one can scrape up from the Old Testament is the call of Isaiah (Is 6:8). The call of an Old Testament prophet should not be regarded as normative for a New Testament missionary. The prophet was sent *to* the people of

God, while the missionary is sent *by* the people of God. It also needs to be established that the "appeal" which Isaiah heard was, in fact, directed indiscriminately to a whole group. Certainly, Old Testament calls depended more upon the subjective certainty of God's calling than upon any call from God's people themselves. More than this, they show considerable variety and do not conform to a pattern. Nehemiah took considerable initiative in seeking information, in praying, and in going himself (Neh 1:2, 4, 11). Ezekiel was already in the place of appointment when he was called (Eze 1:3). Moses' call was not for him to volunteer, but in the form of an inescapable "draft" from which he tried in vain to escape (Ex 3 and 4). It seems gratuitous to make the call of Isaiah typical of all Old Testament calls, let alone to make it a stereotype for the call of New Testament missionaries. The subjective element, however, in the assurance of God's calling to the individual is common to both Old Testament and New Testament calls, but the call in the New Testament has this much larger objective element.

The volunteer system is also suspect on *practical grounds:*

1. When seeking persons for vital positions, one selects the best available. A government does not select ambassadors by calling for volunteers at random. Why should one be any less selective in seeking ambassadors for the King of kings?

2. If you make an emotional appeal at the end of an emotional meeting, the more emotional people are likely to stand up, while more phlegmatic or self-deprecating people who might make better missionaries are unmoved by the emotional appeal and remain sitting down.

3. The disadvantages of the system have then to be overcome by candidates' committees, to weed out all the unsuitable people who have volunteered. This sometimes gives young people problems over guidance: "I feel called, but now the missionary society has turned me down." In practice, we recognize that the subjective conviction of a call is not in itself sufficient.

4. The volunteer system does not produce results. Nearly all missionary societies in all parts of the world claim that they require more recruits. The volunteer system is not producing them.

5. The volunteer system does not produce the kind of missionaries that are required in the proportion in which they are required. There may be a surplus of people volunteering as accountants, secretaries, or nurses, but a serious shortage of doctors, theologians, and most of all, men who are personal soul-winners and church-planters (gifted in starting new congregations).

Both the Bible and common sense, therefore, suggest that the best method is not to call for volunteers but to set up a draft! The most that an individual can do is express his *willingness*. Others must determine his *worthiness*. The individual may be *free* to go, but only his church knows if he is really *fitted* to go.

In fact, the same thing is true within our congregations, for any position of responsibility, even that of being a Sunday school teacher. We all feel so much happier in our own mind when there is a person who is obviously gifted and well qualified for the task, and when those responsible in the church can approach the individual and ask him to consider seriously and prayerfully becoming a Sunday school teacher or superintendent or youth leader or whatever it may be. We always recognize that the ideal is to be able to approach somebody that we already know who is qualified for the task. It is only when the situation becomes desperate that we have to fall back on the less desirable alternative of making a public appeal for volunteers. It is not the best way to do it, but may be the only option left to us. The same is true, I think, of looking for much needed missionaries. We have called for volunteers because the need is desperate. Ideally, though, we would much prefer that people who are already known to be gifted and experienced should be specifically approached in order that they may prayerfully consider the call of the church.

When the church in Jerusalem heard of the need in Antioch, together as a congregation they expressed their sense of responsibility and "They sent Barnabas." He was particularly fitted for the task, because it so happened that he was of the same background as those Cypriots who had been involved with the Cyrenians in initiating the work in Antioch; his very nickname of Barnabas reminds us of his particular gift as an encourager of others (see especially Ac 11:23; 14:22); and he was, we are told in that context, "a good man, full of the Holy Spirit and of faith" (Ac 11:24). They chose the best man they had available for the job.

THE PRACTICAL CONSEQUENCES

The inference is plain that we also should select our "good men" and, as responsible congregations, take the responsibility for selecting and sending them. Instead of the initiative all being left to the individual to approach a missionary society or to approach his own congregation, ministers and congregations together, corporately, should, after prayer, deliberately approach their best, most gifted, and promising Christian workers about the possibility of sending them to places of greater need.

Lest there be any misunderstanding, emphasizing the responsibility of ministers and congregations to take the initiative does not mean any lessening of individual responsibility or an overruling of personal guidance. The individual is still responsible to respond positively or negatively to the congregation's approach. There may be private, personal factors of which the congregation is unaware. Nonetheless, the fact that the individual's subjective sense of call is confirmed by the objective call of the congregation, recognizing his gifts and contribution, reinforces his assurance of the Holy Spirit's guidance. It is certainly true that the Holy Spirit draws the attention of the congregation to individuals, like Saul and Barnabas, whom He has already chosen: "Set apart for Me Barnabas and Saul for the work to which I have called them" (Ac 13:2). Both individuals and the congregation are instructed by the Spirit. There is a dovetailing of the individual's call, the congregation's call to him, and the mission's need.

Under the current system, an individual approaches a missionary society, and frequently the congregation and its elders are not consulted until the individual is already an accepted candidate and an approach is made by the individual or the society in order to gain financial support.

This would seem to be the wrong way around.

Where, on the other hand, the minister and elders have already been involved in making an approach to the individual, the acceptance of responsibility to back up the individual by prayer and giving is immediately implied. It is not now a question of whether the congregation will support the mission's candidate, but whether the mission will accept the church's candidate. The congregation will naturally accept responsibility for one whom they themselves have selected to send out.

It is less compelling to pray for the work of the ABC mission organization in some little known corner of the earth, than it is to pray for our friends William and Mary, well known as enthusiastic members of our congregation, through whom we have been personally blessed and who will be sorely missed as the most gifted leaders of the congregation's work among young people. Of course we will pray for them!

Similarly, we feel no compelling responsibility for missionaries of the ABC mission organization if they are short of money, even those who may have visited our church on their last furlough. On the other hand, we immediately feel a personal responsibility for William and Mary, and are certainly not going to allow them and their children to starve or to be inadequately clothed, because we are directly responsible for sending them out there. They would not be there if we had not sent them, and so we must ensure that they are properly cared for.

Far more, however, than the mere mechanics of all this, because the congregation has been involved in the selection and sending of missionaries, the whole congregation feels far more involved in the particular work which William and Mary are doing. In a very real sense, this is *our* work for which *we* feel responsible, as an extension overseas of *our* own local evangelistic ministry. Thus, while we need to think corporately rather than individualistically, things ought to result in a much greater personal involvement with people we know, rather than the more distant and depersonalized relationship with a missionary organization.

Dr. Arthur Glasser, speaking of the difficulty of getting Christians to be concerned for missions, said,

> If you want to get them to focus on the mission, and then to focus on the church beyond, that takes a great deal of spiritual imagination. This is part of the weakness of the American church in its theological understanding of the missionary enterprise. They have got a poor Doctrine of the Church. Its Doctrine is all on the importance of the individual.[3]

This may be becoming far less true today with the encouraging new emphasis on the body of Christ to be found in many parts of the United States, and yet it is the personal link with William and Mary which personalizes the body of Christ to us, and links us with the church overseas with which they work.

THE ROLE OF THE MISSIONARY SOCIETY

As has already been suggested in the introduction, what we are aiming at is a more vital and dynamic relationship between congregations and missions. We shall need the assistance of the missionary societies in knowing where are the greatest needs and what type and kind of missionary they most urgently require. In the Acts evidence reviewed above, it was plain that not only did the churches take initiative, but so also did those already involved in missionary work in seeking new fellow workers. Barnabas finds Saul. Paul chooses Silas and Timothy.

The missionary societies, from considerable experience, are aware of the various physical and psychological strains and stresses in their particular areas of work, which might exclude someone who might otherwise appear promising. However, the whole emphasis of this suggestion is that, rather than the society making its own selection and presenting the minister and congregation with a fait accompli, the minister and elders at least should be vitally involved from the very beginning. The minister may approach a missionary society representing his congregation on behalf of some potential candidates. (He may need to correspond with a missionary society at an earlier stage to determine the kind of missionary required.) On the other hand, if the furlough missionary thinks that he has found a likely Timothy, he will proceed no further without involving the minister and congregation in his selection.

It is those who have known the candidate for a

number of years in his own local church situation who are the best qualified to judge whether he has a contribution to make or not (Ac 16:1-2). It is difficult for a missionary executive to tell from the candidate's own completed papers and a short personal interview whether the individual has a *contribution* to make. Will he really be used to save souls and catalyze new congregations? The fact that he may have been trained in Bible college or seminary indicates only that he has been trained; it says little about aptitudes or gifts. A far greater involvement of the congregation in selection would serve to eliminate some of those unhappy cases where young people go overseas as missionaries and are subsequently found to be fruitless misfits. There is however one possible snag here.

It is not always easy for a small congregation to be sufficiently objective: they may be starry-eyed about their own protégé. All their eager geese are alleged to be effective swans! The missionary society is able to compare the caliber of candidates from other churches and other countries, and provides an objective check upon overoptimistic evaluations of some congregation's local blue-eyed boy.

Let us just pause at this point and consider who are the best qualified people in our own congregation by virtue of their gifts, training, and experience to serve as overseas missionaries. Do we have "a good man"—a Barnabas, a Saul, a Mark, or a Timothy? Should not the minister and congregation together seek the guidance of the Holy Spirit in determining who are those whom He would have us set apart for the work to which He has called them?

2

How Can the Missionary's Furlough Best Be Spent?

Ministers and congregations have a crucial responsibility for the retraining and encouraging of furlough missionaries.

THE CURRENT CONVENTION called "furlough" needs to be closely scrutinized. Particularly, our curious custom of "deputation" needs to be objectively reconsidered. Many missionaries spend their furlough engaged in the rat race known as deputation, apparently "planned more in terms of the maximum number of meetings rather than in a considered strategy of arousing involvement and interest."[1] And again, "The missionary is still involved in mental fatigue, high travelling expenses, and, towards the end, staleness of repetition."[2] Far too often the missionaries repeat the same two or three messages again and again; their presentations tend to become stereotyped and stale; and they themselves become tired and weary, from both travel and "representing their mission."

24

(These statements might be regarded as exaggerated, but they are often nearer the truth than we may imagine.)

It is highly questionable whether such deputation is in the best interests either of the missionary himself, or of the congregations who have to listen to him. Apart from the fact that it has become habitual, why does the missionary have to dash around like this? Partly because this is what his missionary society apparently expects him to do, and the congregations are becoming resigned to his doing; but also, let's face it, with an eye to financial support. Inconsistently perhaps, the so-called faith missions no less than others recognize that the interest of congregations must be maintained if investment in missionary work is to continue. If the sending church were fully bearing his support, then it would not really be necessary for him to go on this soul-destroying round of meetings. Certainly the EMA Survey is not alone in questioning whether deputation as currently practiced is the proper use of the missionary "to foster and sustain the churches' participation in worldwide mission at an acceptable and personal level."[3]

A BIBLICAL PATTERN

It is not without significance that, when Paul and Barnabas returned from their first term of service in Cyprus and Galatia to the congregation "from which they had been commended by the grace of God for the work that they had accomplished," they not only gathered the church together and "began to report all things that God had done with them and how He had opened the door of faith to the Gentiles" (Ac 14:26-27), but it specifically and perhaps rather pointedly, in view of our contrary practices, states that they spent "not a little" time with the disciples (v. 28, marg.). How wonderful it is when modern furlough missionaries are permitted by their missions to do just this! Would that more home churches insisted upon it!

A PRACTICAL ILLUSTRATION

Recently, some missionary friends of mine, after a rather discouraging term of service with a struggling emerging congregation in Japan, spent practically the whole of their furlough with a particular congregation in north London and were provided with housing in the area. The husband was accepted as a kind of assistant pastor. The minister generously shared his pulpit with him and made tactful suggestions for the improvement of his imperfect homiletics! The missionary and his wife not only were regularly in the congregation, but took active part in work among young people and in outreach among young married couples. This was a tonic for the hitherto discouraged missionaries who received all the benefits of being involved in the life of a spiritually thriving and vital fellowship of Christians. They returned to the field better qualified to give pastoral help and teaching to Japanese fellow believers.

Contrast, too, the difference between their relationship with this congregation and that of the weekend visitor on deputation. Doubtless if the deputationist's presentation is very striking, some of the message may be remembered still on the following Sunday; but probably most people will have forgotten most of it long before the deputationist returns to the field. By contrast, my two friends are now personally known on first-name terms to most people in the congregation. Some people there were led to the Lord through them; others were personally blessed by their advice and testimony. Others feel closer to them because they befriended the missionaries. The congregation is aware of some of the human failings of my friends and therefore want to pray for them and their work now, because they know that they need praying for! There is far less compulsion to pray for the relatively impersonal stranger on deputation, who spoke about (they can't quite remember what) a couple of years back. The congregation now feels personally involved through my friends with the Lord's work in northern Japan.

Isn't this a much better way of spending furlough? Isn't this a far greater benefit both to the missionary and to the congregation? And does

it not give a far greater satisfaction to the minister,
to know that he has made a very real contribution
to work overseas through the help that he was
able to give to this particular missionary family?
Not only has he enjoyed fellowship in the work
with him and had the assistance of a colleague,
thus encompassing more work than he could ever
have done on his own, but also he has enhanced
the ministry of the missionary and sent him back
more encouraged and more effective than when
he first went abroad.

I was encouraged to discover that the senti-
ments expressed above are, if anything, stated
even more strongly in *Abroad from at Home*. The
question is posed: "How much of a missionary's
furlough should be spent actually living in the
vicinity of his supporting church, enabling him
and his family to participate completely in church
life? One week? Six months? The full year?"[4]
And subsequently, the answer to this question is
given: "Opportunities for deeper missionary-sup-
porter relationships would exist if missionaries
stayed longer with an individual church—perhaps
at one church for the whole of their furlough.
This is scriptural, economical for the societies,
practical for the missionaries, illuminating for the
church, and beneficial to all concerned."[5] It is
pointed out that in the United Kingdom's situation, "The missionary who has a church with an
overseas orientated outlook supporting him is one

of the fortunate few. Yet even such a church is highly unlikely to see more than a passing glimpse of their missionary when he is home on furlough."[6] Another point taken is that whereas 64 percent of furlough ministry was arranged by the missionary society, only 3 percent was arranged by the missionary's own church. While the North American situation is much more healthy than this, churches vary tremendously in the extent to which they are prepared to involve the furlough missionary in active ministry with his home congregation. While it is true that he may often be away because his speaking is appreciated elsewhere, it is sometimes true that he is away because his home congregation does not appreciate him enough!

Many missionaries, in the interests of getting to the field earlier in order to adapt better and learn the language faster, may go abroad with a minimum of church experience. It is far more profitable for them and the emerging churches with which they are working overseas, for the missionaries to spend their furlough being better fitted to fulfill a pastoral teaching ministry, than for them to hawk around the country two or three rather tired and shabby messages about "our work" or "our mission." Putting this more positively, an enthusiastic home church and its minister may be able to make an enormous contribution to missionary work through the experience in a thriving church life that they can give and the enthusiasm that they can generate by ensuring the maximum possible involvement of the furlough missionary in the church's ministry.

I am not implying by this that I think missionaries should necessarily be totally supported by one congregation, though Dr. George Peters makes a good case for this:

> A local congregation should accept first and full financial responsibility for the missionaries of its own church. The churches do so for their pastors and they should do likewise for their missionaries. A partial or token monthly support can hardly be justified morally or Scripturally, and it dislocates and disinherits a rightful member of the church by making him or her a member at large and a debtor to several churches and at times to numerous individuals. Thus the church home of the missionary is disrupted.[7]

He does however modify this somewhat when he says, "Local congregations should accept a larger share of a few missionaries than a small portion of a larger number of missionaries."

Regarding furlough he suggests,

> A local congregation should continue the missionary on the payroll while on furlough, provide for him a home, help to re-establish him and his family in the congregation and arrange with the society to engage him or her in a min-

istry in relation to the home church, either on full or part-time basis.^x

While the missionary may have been brought up or converted through one congregation, he may have become involved in another during professional or Bible training. More than this, he probably has a relationship with his wife's home church as well. Evangelical churches serving university communities probably have more potential missionaries than they could hope to support on their own.

Moreover, I am not suggesting that all deputation should stop. If this were so, some smaller congregations might go for very considerable periods without ever hearing news of missionary work in other parts of the world. Really vital telling of what the Lord is doing overseas may bring tremendous blessing and encouragement to devoted Christians in remoter rural areas. Obviously *some* deputation work must continue in order to bring news to other congregations of what the Lord is doing in many other places. Even if one congregation is supporting a number of missionaries, they need to have a much wider knowledge of the Lord's working than acquaintance with that number of missionaries can ever possibly provide. It would be unfortunate if we swung from the extreme of too much travelling around to far too little, so that there was a dearth of missionary information for worldwide prayer coverage.

Such bringing of information is also scriptural; thus Paul sent Tychicus:

> That you also may know about my circum-
> stances, how I am doing, Tychicus, the beloved
> brother and faithful minister in the Lord, will
> make everything known to you. And I have
> sent him to you for this very purpose, *so that*
> *you may know about us,* and that he may com-
> fort your hearts (Eph 6:21-22, italics mine).

The missionary may in fact fulfill this responsibility of informing other congregations far better,
and they may listen the more when everybody
knows that he is not doing it in order to get their
money!

The emphasis that I am suggesting here is that
missionaries, while they ought not to discontinue
visiting other churches to a certain extent in order
to bring them news, should spend far less time
itinerating and far more time in a settled church
situation, preferably with the congregation which
first selected them and sent them out.

Again *Abroad from at Home* underlines this
conclusion: "The number of one night 'missionary
stands' should be drastically reduced. These are
largely ineffective in achieving the kind of support
Societies need. Programmes can be filled much
more easily by the Society sending a filmstrip or
slideset," and they urge that "the whole subject
of the missionary's use of furlough and his deputa-

tion ministry during it needs urgent attention by all Societies" and "a careful and immediate review of deputation programmes is indicated, with a concentrated effort being made to encourage churches and missionaries to be in close contact for longer periods during furlough."[9]

The stress, however, that I would like to make is that here is another ministry for pastors and congregations—retreading tired missionaries! A tremendous contribution overseas can be made next year by a missionary who has benefited this year from the pastor's tutoring and the congregation's education, resulting in a greater mutual involvement and enthusiasm.

3

Who Sparks the Churches' Interest in Missions?

Ministers and elders have the central responsibility for ensuring that missions are a principal passion of their congregations (and not a peripheral program for the super saints).

IN MANY CONGREGATIONS, missions are a sideshow—and a rather dull and insignificant sideshow at that. Such churches can be identified by listening to the announcements: "Wednesday night, the church prayer meeting; Thursday night, the women's sewing circle; Friday night, the missionary prayer meeting." The implication is that the few old dears who are interested in sewing can get on with it. And the following evening, those (and it is probably the same few old dears, the Lord bless them) who are enthusiastic about praying for missions can get on with that. But it is a peripheral activity, and probably nobody would be more surprised than the minister if many people started turning up. "It is sad but true that one missionary meeting in three is held mid-week when usually less than a quarter of a church's membership turns out. And those who do turn out are mostly the elderly and the already interested."[1] The recent Ascot Survey in Britain, seeking to discover the most common attitudes to missionary work, was more than horrified to discover that "23% thought it was an optional extra for those who had time, 21% thought it was a duty but rather a nuisance, while 16% felt that missionary work was no longer the concern of the Western Church."[2]

In other words—let's face it—in such congregations, missions are regarded as an unimportant, peripheral sideshow. After all, why not?

I would hasten to add that I am not suggesting that missions should be central rather than peripheral merely because this is the particular ax which I am grinding. I want to make this emphasis because I believe it to be biblical and in the greatest interests both of the sending congregation itself and of the whole church of Jesus Christ. We all long for a revitalizing of the sense of participation in God's work overseas on the part of our congregations at home. "The aim should be to make overseas missionary work a natural and inescapable part of local church life for *all* the church members."[3]

A Biblical Emphasis

Let me support my assertion that it is biblical. The Great Commission makes it clear that *every baptized believer* (and therefore the whole church and therefore each local congregation) *has been called* to make disciples of all nations. The missionary calling is the concern of the whole church. It is not just a few super saints who have been called, but rather everyone who has been discipled and baptized in the name of the Father, the Son, and the Holy Spirit, is to be taught to obey everything that Christ commanded us (Mt 28:19); and among these commands, the one which comes to us with greatest force is the final one delivered in this very context, namely, to go and make disciples of all nations. The whole church therefore is a missionary church, and therefore, every congregation should be a missionary congregation. I am not suggesting that evangelism at home and overseas is the *only* reason for the church's existence, for this would be to ignore other biblical emphases. But it is one of the two or three main functions and ministries of the church to be fulfilled until Christ returns.

It is, however, one thing to recognize this intellectually and another to put it into practice. It is one thing for a minister to determine to make overseas missions central in his church program and another thing to get his whole congregation enthused and involved in it. How do you do it?

The EA Report talks of a "massive re-education job" needing to be done.[1] We all recognize the difficulty of that task, but is it not really worth doing?

Too Many Missions Muddle

At this point, it is freely admitted that we missionary societies have confused the picture for the churches and for ourselves because there are too many of us. There are so many interdenominational missions that if a congregation were to give us all in succession an opportunity to take the annual missionary weekend, we should all get a turn about twice in a century which would not do either us or you much good! There are far too many missionary magazines, and in the average congregation, no one person has time to sort out the wheat from the chaff and to present a readily digestible digest of information which will enable the congregation to feel fully involved in the worldwide growth of the church.

Could we simplify it for you in some way?

We are trying. In North America, the Co-operation and Comity Committee of the IFMA has the current specific objective of reducing the total number of evangelical mission organizations by means of merger, amalgamation, or absorption. In Britain the report of the Evangelical Alliance Commission on World Mission quoted above says:

As we have seen, much closer co-operation, if not complete amalgamation, will be almost essential. We suggest that the pattern we should aim at is to have far fewer societies, in two groups: (a) *Missions that concentrate on geographical areas*. It could be the best plan to have just one evangelical missionary society each for, say, the Indian sub-continent, East Asia, Latin America, Sub-Saharan Africa, the Middle East and North Africa, and Europe; though some of these areas might be divided. (b) *Missions that concentrate on specialist functions*, acting as service agencies in fields such as radio and television, literature, leprosy work, youth work and so on. We wondered if there should be a third group, of denominational missions, and were undecided. The resources available might be deployed very much better through missions in one of these other groups.[5]

There is thus increasing encouragement to act on the urge to merge. "There seems little doubt that the multiplicity of missions is a factor in the decline in missionary support in Britain. . . . Three church leaders in four of those who replied to the Ascot Survey felt that there should be some amalgamation of societies." It is significant that "81% of UK Christian students surveyed said they would prefer some amalgamation of societies holding the same basic beliefs, working in the same part of the world or in the same type of work."[6]

However, there is no need for congregations to

wait until we missions have put our house in order before aiming at a deeper involvement. There are far too many missionary societies for each of us to have our own prayer meeting even in the very largest congregations.

A Practical Possibility

When I was a student, we had a slogan to the effect that each mature Christian should know "something about everywhere, and everything about somewhere." This means, in effect, that we expected a general interest by every Christian in things going on all over the world; but we recognized, in addition, the practical necessity of a special focus on churches and missionaries in a limited geographical area. Therefore, we established a system of small, informal missionary prayer groups. In a small congregation, five or six continent-wide groups may be the best that can be done, but ideally it seems better to focus attention on smaller areas. Such groups provide for a maximum participation of members. There are so many different missionary magazines that each member may take a different one; and each receive the regular prayer circulars of three or four different missionaries. Thus on every occasion when such a group meets together for prayer, each is able to provide a few meaningful topics which he himself has gleaned.

Alternatively, instead of dividing the groups'

prayer focus and responsibility by geographical areas, there could be divisions sociologically; such as, students' or young people's work, radio and television, medical and relief work, literature publishing and distribution, and evangelism and church planting.[7]

The inauguration of such a system of *congregationally sponsored* prayer groups with the wholehearted encouragement of the minister could change the whole picture and produce a deeper involvement in world missions than has ever been achieved by allowing missions to be the sole preserve of the congregation's most enthusiastic fringe. Just as in North America all the adults and young people are expected to be involved in the Sunday school classes which meet before the main Sunday morning worship service, so every church member ought to be expected to belong to one of the missionary prayer groups.

Here are several of the advantages:

1. Each group provides a particular focus for prayer letters from missionaries working in what has been adopted by the group as "our area."
2. Each group provides a particular focus for deputation speakers visiting from that part of the world.
3. All of the groups can be further encouraged and strengthened through contact with inter-

national students from the area being prayed for.

4. Members of the groups may be encouraged to visit the country of their group's interest. In these days of increasing international travel, students often travel on summer vacations, and retired people take world tours for which they have saved for many years. The ease of world travel and television coverage which has brought us into McLuhan's "Global Village" makes it much easier for us to be involved in missions than it was for our grandparents.

5. Members of prayer groups can be alerted when documentary films on their areas of interest are being shown.

6. The groups may take responsibility for missionary exhibits, which then become not sideshows run by missionary executives and deputationists but a further opportunity for the participation of the whole congregation in expressing their involvement by creating their own displays.*

*Some of the best ideas that I have come across for helping the missionary involvement of congregations are found in the publication *Perspective,* produced by the OMF/BMMF jointly in London for those responsible for the missionary emphasis in youth programs. The ideas, however, are often equally valid for adult programs and can be applied far more widely geographically than for the particular East and West Asian interests they represent.

Not only does such involvement by small groups encourage a far more active participation by a far greater number, rather than mere passive spectating of missionary visitors, but such small group activity is in itself a blessing to the congregation. We ought surely to be concerned by the present discontent and dissatisfaction with our current practice. It would be helpful from time to time to invite the secretaries of missionary societies in whose work the particular church has an interest to come and talk over ways of achieving closer personal communication between church members and missionaries. We know that some people may be turned off by societies, but what are we really, but a group of Christian individuals associated together in the Lord's work overseas, often in difficult circumstances and desperately needing the assurance that there are dedicated Christians at home involved personally by praying for us in depth and backing us up in many other ways?

4

Should Ministers Ever Consider Missionary Service?

Ministers who are experienced pastors/teachers have a certain responsibility to consider missionary service themselves.

IT CANNOT ESCAPE the attention of a careful reader of the New Testament that those who were sent out as missionaries by those first-century congregations were themselves already experienced Christian workers. It was the two leading workers in the church at Antioch, Saul and Barnabas, who went forth (Ac 13:1-2). Silas was already a leading man among the brethren (Ac 15:22) and a prophet (Ac 15:32), before Paul chose him as a fellow worker. Even though Timothy was much younger, it is not without significance that he was "well spoken of by the brethren" not only in his own home congregation at Lystra but in Iconium as well (Ac 16:2).

In other words, those chosen to be missionaries in the New Testament churches were ministers already. This would suggest that, when we are seeking to discover which person in our congregations might have the greatest contribution to make overseas, the person concerned is probably not some presently insignificant student attending a Bible college but rather someone who is already prominent and active as a leader in the work of your congregation. It is someone you would all miss. If they are to make a contribution in another culture, we must be certain first that they are able to make an effective contribution in their own.

If you won't miss them, we don't want them!

Send us your cream, not your dregs. This means that in the larger type of congregations, as in many North American churches, with a team ministry and a row of assistant ministers, the most likely person for you to send is one of them!

THE NEED FOR PASTORS

In many countries overseas today, the greatest lack is missionaries with considerable church pastoral experience who are able to train and help national ministers to grapple with their own local problems.

The chief work of missions is the planting, propagating, and perfecting of congregations. This is what missionary work is all about. Who will do it better than those who already have considerable congregational experience?

In Japan, there are frequently tiny congregations which seem to get stuck at a membership of around fifty or so. There are understandable cultural reasons for this, but a man who can teach a national pastor how to delegate and encourage the ministry of others could have a fruitful ministry in the Japanese churches. In Korea, many of the churches are failing to reach the younger generation and are asking, "Send us men of experience to help reach and keep our young people." In Indonesia, ministers may have had as much as five years' theological training, but a great deal of this has been doctrinal and theoretical and weak on the pastoral side. Such a man can flounder desperately when he finds himself expected to minister to a congregation of 5,000 or more scattered in smaller congregations across a wide area. A missionary with experience in administering and pastoring larger congregations has a real contribution to make. In Taiwan, among the tribal churches, in one tribe alone there are more than 10,000 believers organized into fifty congregations with only some ten ministers. These are just a few among many places where a great contribution could be made by men with pastoral experience.

Experienced pastors, then, with considerable church experience, provided they are young enough to learn a language and adaptable enough to move with their families to an entirely different cultural environment, could make a far greater contribution than a recent product of a Bible college. There are areas of the world which are glad to take such younger workers and train them there. There are other places where the national church has gained considerably in strength, where their greatest need is more experience. You might be used in one of those. You may have to twist your congregation's arm hard to persuade them to release you: all the more likely then that you have a contribution to make. There is little doubt, if missionary work is central in your church and the whole congregation has been aroused to fulfill its responsibility to make disciples of all nations, that your ministry will be wonderfully supported by the prayers and deep sense of personal involvement of those who have already been blessed through your ministry.

If you yourself are not young enough to go, you could make it your prayerful aim to train your assistant ministers and the lay leaders of your congregation—just as Charles Simeon trained Henry Martyn—and to impart to them your pastoral experience that they might be the ones who actually go. But it could be you!

Conclusion

IT IS MY CONVICTION that if we were able to implement suggestions such as these involving the whole congregation in the selection, sending, training, and praying for missionaries, missionary deputation would cease to be a bore and a drag for ministers and churches, and a distraction from the main work of the congregation.

If we were able to mobilize and involve our whole congregation in such an enthusiastic missions program, it could deepen our whole consciousness of involvement in the body of Christ. Christians in our congregations are missing an exciting privilege if they are deprived of the fullest possible involvement in the task of proclaiming Jesus as Lord and of making disciples of all nations.

We often talk of the work of missionaries as being costly and sacrificial, although we who are missionaries would rather stress what a privilege it is and what blessing we receive. It is less often appreciated that involvement by congregations and their ministers at home also can be costly in the midst of their busy lives, in terms of time given to keeping up with developments and speeding forward these developments through prayer. It is, however, also gloriously true, correspondingly, that it is a privilege as well as a duty and brings the greatest blessing to those who find the greatest involvement.

Notes

INTRODUCTION

1. *Abroad from at Home,* Summary of Ascot Surveys (London: Evangelical Missions Assoc., 1971), p. 15.
2. "Erasing the Old Image" in *Fiftieth Annual Meeting Study Papers* (IFMA, 1967).
3. *One World, One Task,* Report of the Evangelical Alliance Commission on World Missions, 1971, p. 155.

CHAPTER 1

1. "The Missionary: Do You Know Who Sends Him?" *Africa Now,* Nov.-Dec. 1970, p. 5.
2. George H. Slavin, "Missionary Deputation in N. America Today" (Report delivered at OMF meeting, Philadelphia), p. 5.
3. Quoted in ibid.

CHAPTER 2

1. *EMA Ascot Survey Summary* (London: Evangelical Alliance), p. 24.
2. *Abroad from at Home,* p. 3.
3. Ibid., p. 18.
4. Ibid., p. 5.
5. Ibid., p. 16.
6. Ibid., p. 4.
7. "Towards Co-operation" in *Fiftieth Annual Meeting Study Papers* (IFMA, 1967).
8. Ibid.
9. *Abroad from at Home,* p. 16.

CHAPTER 3

1. *Abroad from at Home,* p. 6.
2. *EMA Ascot Survey Summary,* p. 6.
3. *Abroad from at Home,* p. 17.
4. *One World, One Task,* p. 150.
5. Ibid., p. 140.
6. *EMA Ascot Survey Summary,* p. 13.
7. Suggested in *One World, One Task,* p. 156.